Words by Robin Feiner

Aa

A is for Andy Reid.
With multiple clutch Super Bowl victories and a staggering tally of wins, coach Reid is the genius behind a legendary dynasty.
No doubt about it, 'Big Red' is the greatest coach in Kansas City history!

B
78

B is for Bobby Bell.
This All-Pro linebacker is one of the most athletic defensive players ever. He helped lead the Chiefs to Super Bowl IV, and he's still tied for the NFL record for most interceptions returned for touchdowns by a linebacker.

61

Cc

C is for Curley Culp.
The 1975 Defensive Player of the Year was a menace on the field. He's probably one of the greatest nose tackles ever, and he helped Kansas City dominate Minnesota in Super Bowl IV. Chiefs legend, indeed!

58
D
58

D is for Derrick Thomas.
From the moment he stepped into Arrowhead in 1989, D.T. terrorized opposing offenses. He still holds the record for most sacks in a game with 7 and the most sacks in Chiefs history with 126.5. Greatest Chiefs defensive player ever? You bet.

18

E is for Emmitt Thomas.
This All-Pro was a legend on the field and the sidelines. He recorded a whopping 58 career interceptions before becoming a tough-nosed defensive coach. In 2019, he finally retired from the game he loves, still as a KC Chief.

84
84

Ff

F is for Fred Arbanas. Some of the best tight ends in NFL history have played for KC — and that all started with Fred. Arbanas racked up 198 career receptions and 3,101 yards, both Chiefs tight end records for a time. No wonder he's in the Missouri Sports Hall of Fame.

88

G is for Tony Gonzalez.
For 12 incredible years,
Gonzalez was the Chiefs best
player. With insane route running
and jaw-dropping catches, he
became a 14-time Pro Bowler and
6-time All-Pro. And he still holds
many records for tight ends today.

H is for Hank Stram.
In 1960, the Dallas Texans were a second-rate AFL team. This legend took over as coach, and the soon-to-be Kansas City Chiefs never looked back. By 1974, the Chiefs had moved over to the NFL and won their first Super Bowl.

10

I is for Isiah Pacheco.
This running back who 'runs like he bites people' came into the NFL in 2022 and took over the Kansas City backfield. With a knack for contact and speed like a gazelle, he's helped the Chiefs become a dynasty. Talk about a start to a career!

95

J is for Chris Jones.
‘Stone Cold Jones’ is an absolute force. At a towering 6′6″, he plows through offensive linemen. And with more than 80 career sacks, he’s a big reason the Chiefs have dominated the NFL this century.

31
K

Kk

K is for Kevin Ross.
This legend played 10 standout seasons for KC. He hounded opposing wide receivers with his tight bump-and-run coverage, snagging two Pro Bowl nods along the way. In 2011, he was inducted into the Chiefs Hall of Honor.

63

L is for Willie Lanier.
Next to Bobby Bell, Lanier helped form one of the greatest linebacker tandems ever. His crowning moment came in '69, when he led the Chiefs to a goal-line stand against the Jets that landed them in the Super Bowl.

15

Mm

M is for Patrick Mahomes.
With a handful of Super Bowl rings and a long list of accolades and awards, Mahomes is the most talented QB we've ever seen. He doesn't just throw touchdown passes, he throws fireballs.
Will he catch Tom Brady as the greatest quarterback ever?
Only time will tell.

90
90

Nn

N is for **N**eil Smith.
Known for his seven-foot wingspan, Smith was a legendary game-wrecker. His most dominant stretch came between '92 and '95, when he terrorized the league with 53 sacks and helped the Chiefs to six straight playoff appearances.

89
89

O is for Otis Taylor.
This high-flying Chiefs legend was one of the greatest receivers ever to lace 'em up. During an All-Pro career, he hauled in 7,306 yards and 57 touchdowns. As his QB Len Dawson said, 'If you got the pass to Otis, you knew he'd catch it.'

31

P is for **P**riest Holmes.
Though he went undrafted in '97, Holmes quickly became a legend. In '03, he scored a whopping 27 touchdowns, an NFL record at the time. These days, he's considered the greatest Chiefs RB ever to live.

11
10
16
16
Q

Q is for Great Chiefs Quarterbacks. Before Mahomes, the Chiefs had a long line of stud QBs. Len Dawson won KC their first ever Super Bowl, while Trent Green and Alex Smith consistently led the team to victory. They were all clutch, and they're all Chiefs legends.

R
42
42

R is for Johnny Robinson.
In the '60s and '70s, this Hall of Famer was a true terror, snatching opposing passes left, right, and center. During the '69 season, when the Chiefs won Super Bowl IV, he led the team with eight interceptions; the following year, he led the entire league with 10!

S is for Steve Spagnuolo. 'Coach Spags' is a mastermind. He's coached many Chiefs defenses, but the best was the 2023–24 version that became the NFL's most dominant. With a victory in Super Bowl LVIII, Spags became the first coordinator ever to win four Super Bowls.

10
10

T is for Tyreek 'Cheetah' Hill. With 67 regular season touchdowns in his Chiefs days, the NFL's most agile and exciting wide receiver ran circles around opposing defenses. In Super Bowl LIV, Cheetah came up with the most clutch play of the game: a 44-yard catch that spurred KC to victory.

U is for 2023 Underdogs. Under Coach Reid, the Chiefs are often the favorites — but in '23, KC entered the playoffs as underdogs. Led by Mahomes, Kelce, and a vicious defense, they ripped off four straight victories, ending with an epic win in Super Bowl LVIII.

V is for Brett Veach.
With Veach as GM, the Chiefs have won several Super Bowls. But his greatest achievement came when he urged Kansas City to draft a little-known QB out of Texas Tech named Patrick Mahomes. The rest is history.

68

W is for Will Shields. Throughout 14 seasons, this Hall of Famer never missed a game while blocking for the likes of Holmes, Marcus Allen, and Larry Johnson. Nowadays, he's regarded as the greatest Chiefs offensive lineman ever.

82

Xx

X is for Dante 'X-Factor' Hall. They called this legend 'X-Factor' and 'The Human Joystick' because at any moment, he could take it to the house. With his dazzling jukes and blazing speed, he once scored kickoff return touchdowns in four straight games, still an NFL record.

Y is for 44 Yards.
The '13 Seconds' game was one of the greatest matchups ever. Just when all hope seemed lost for the Chiefs, Mahomes completed two quick passes to travel 44 yards and tie up the game. In overtime, he hit Travis Kelce for the game-winning TD.

Z
87

Z is for Travis 'Zeus' Kelce. With multiple Super Bowl rings, a long list of receiving records, and the most swagger of any player in the league, Kelce has cemented himself as a legend. His teammates might call him Zeus, but he's also the greatest tight end in the NFL.

The ever-expanding legendary library

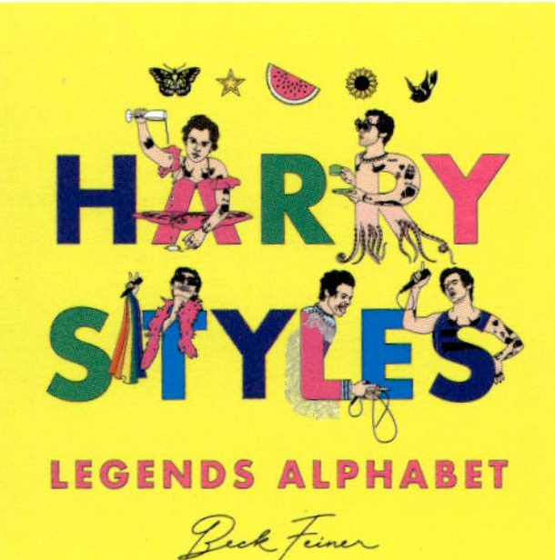

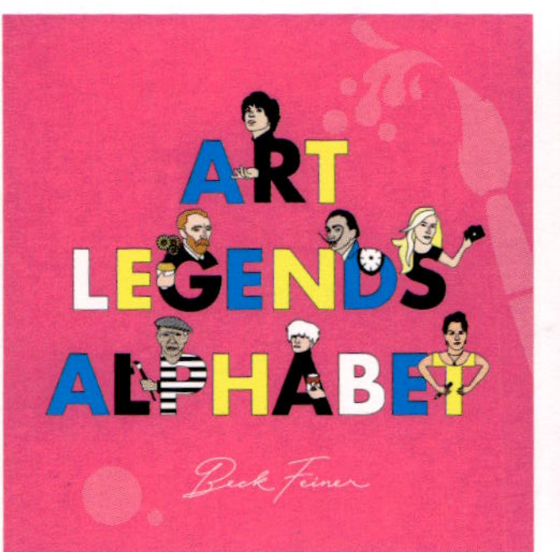

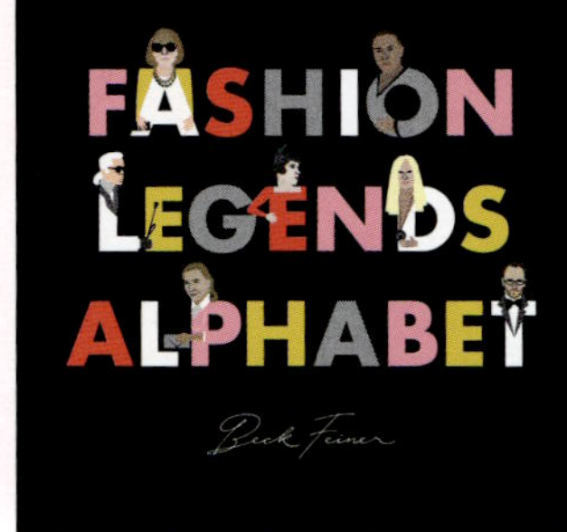

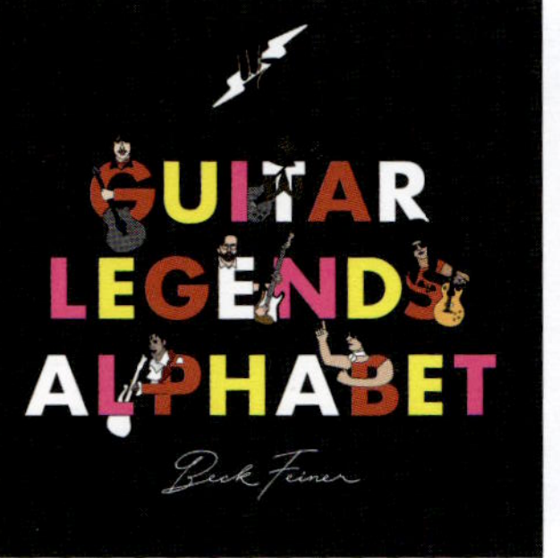

EXPLORE THESE LEGENDARY ALPHABETS & MORE AT WWW.ALPHABETLEGENDS.COM

CHIEFS LEGENDS ALPHABET

www.alphabetlegends.com

Published by Alphabet Legends Pty Ltd in 2024
Created by Beck Feiner

Printed and bound in China.

9780975669259